The James Bond Cold Reading
A re-imagining of the 'classic' reading

Amazon Print edition

Includes 10 Flash Cards
See download link at end of book

Table Of Contents

Foreword

I am confident that this book won't make you another expert in cold reading. Instead of that, I know this book can effectively turn you into an actual cold reader.

This book deals with a very specific form of cold reading: the delivery of stock phrases, or stock readings. Building on the successful systematization for learning Palmistry that he already shared with the community, Julian Moore is undertaking in this book the not so easy task of giving you the right pointers to do a stock reading that will come out in your own words.

Stock readings are applied fiction. A well selected plot that you offer to a person, suggesting directly and indirectly that such plot IS the person. After all, each one of us is a crossroad of tales and myths looking for a way to realize themselves. Each one of us is a tale writing itself. "Society" can be defined as a group of people sharing the same tales. Know the society's tale and you will know the people who live in that society.

James Bond movies aren't successful because we all want to be like James Bond, but because James Bond is like all of us. Several times along his adventures we find ourselves in the same mindset as Bond. There is a part of Bond that is human, and is his human side that makes his heroic side worthwhile. This is what Julian has capitalized upon - a systematic approach to understanding a basic and well tested story-line, so you can use it in a way that makes sense and comes out naturally.

Half of what you need to perform powerful cold reading is an understanding of the story-lines that define human nature. The other half is confidence. No one but yourself will give you the later, but Julian can help you with the former. That is why he wrote this book. It's a good thing that you are reading it now!

A little suggestion: don't bother by peeking at your participant's shoes, shopping bags, rings, or fingernails. Forget about picking clues in the way Sherlock Holmes famously did. There is nothing to see in your participant since the effect we call cold reading, when we are using stock lines, isn't something you do to them, but something you help them to do by themselves. Don't force it, LET IT HAPPEN! What you are really doing is offering the person a piece of information in a context that suggest that this information is about her. Therefore, is up to the person's mind to define the relevance of the information you are delivering. Cold reading is real and powerful magic, because it is magic that happens in the participant's mind. You are giving them permission to re-create themselves through your words. Practice that skill with respect.

There is something intriguing, entertaining, and potentially enlightening in knowing how are we perceived by others. That is why cold reading is so powerful. A performer capable of doing that will always command his audience's attention.

But you know that! Otherwise you wouldn't be reading this book, seduced by the allure that cold reading has over all kind of mystery performers.

So, are you ready for your mission? Get into the action and remember that if you stand confident under fire, the bullets won't harm you. The party is on. It is time for you to make your move...

Enrique Enriquez.
New York, April 2007

3

Introduction

The original 'Classic Reading' is a list of twelve truisms that can be said to apply to almost anyone. Dating back to the 1940's, these 'stock' lines can be used to either supplement an already know reading system such as palmistry, or to add interest to a mentalist effect where there is a need to 'say something' appropriate to give the impression that more is known about a person that is otherwise apparent.

When approaching 'Cold Reading', these twelve lines are usually the first thing the novice mentalist or reader stumbles across in the search for the easiest way to appear to know about people with little effort. However, on attempting to commit these lines to memory it becomes quickly apparent that they are not only quite hard to remember, but are woefully out of context.

My answer to this dilemma is to base the entire classic reading around the famous James Bond character. By applying the twelve truisms to certain facets of a character that most of us feel that we know already, we have a chance to not only learn the lines quickly, but more importantly understand the ideas behind the lines and therefore expand on these ideas in some broader context.

I am not a fan of 'stock lines' per se, but I do understand the need for some people to be 'ready to go' with little notice, and for others to be able to bolster their own readings for those occasional moments when inspiration runs dry. The 'James Bond Cold Reading' is a memory aid as well as a visualization tool to help words come more easily.

This ebook is divided into three sections:

> • **Section One** deals with the work involved in committing the lines of The James Bond Cold Reading to memory.
>
> • **Section Two** deals with the use of these lines to deliver a reading either as a stand alone system or in conjunction with an effect.
>
> • **Section Three** show how the principles used in The James Bond Cold Reading can be expanded upon.

As with my previous book 'Speed Learning Palmistry ~ Palm Readings In Your Own Words' there are flash cards to accompany The James Bond Cold Reading that you can print out and take with you wherever you go, allowing you to practice whenever you have a spare moment. However, there are two sets of flash cards this time - one set which deals with the James Bond Cold Reading only, and another set which is purposefully left with spaces for you to fill in your own characters, ideas and stock lines.

The flash cards print easily onto 6X4 inch index cards and if you do them a few at a time it is easy to print them out on both sides with your printer setting on portrait.

This book may appear to be long but in fact the concepts are extremely easy to use

All you have to do is remember twelve lines and learn how to make them work for you and you're already on the way

By creating a plot using the James Bond character to join the ideas of the twelve lines together you will be remembering them far quicker than you thought possible so you can spend more time actually using them!

Use the flash cards provided and learn the lines in hours not days!

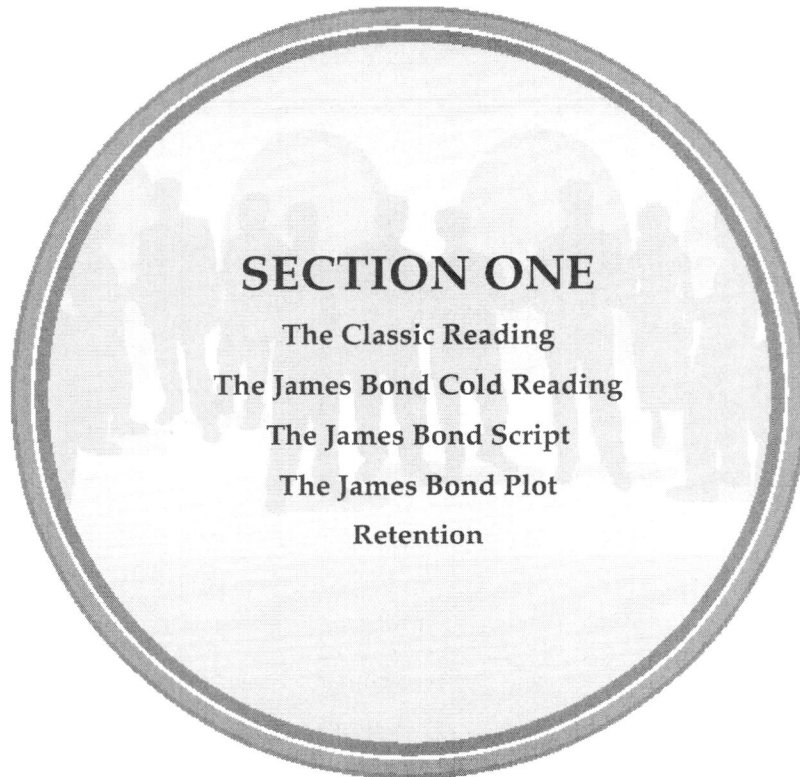

SECTION ONE

The Classic Reading

The James Bond Cold Reading

The James Bond Script

The James Bond Plot

Retention

The 'Classic' Reading

The 'Classic Reading' as it's become known is a list of twelve phrases that most people would agree applied to them. In tests over the years these twelve truisms have been found to be 'correct' when used on people at least 80% of the time. It's not hard to see why this might be the case, but to simply deliver these lines as they stand isn't going to make most people see you as having any kind of empathy or insight.

1. At times you are extroverted, affable, sociable, while at other times you are introverted, wary, and reserved.
2. You have a strong need for other people to like you and for them to admire you.
3. Disciplined and controlled on the outside, you tend to be worrisome and insecure on the inside.
4. You have a tendency to be critical of yourself.
5. You pride yourself on being an independent thinker and do not accept others' opinions without satisfactory proof.
6. You have found it unwise to be too frank in revealing yourself to others.
7. Your sexual adjustment has presented some problems for you.
8. While you have some personality weaknesses, you are generally able to compensate for them.
9. At times you have serious doubts as to whether you have made the right decision or done the right thing.
10. You prefer a certain amount of change and variety and become dissatisfied when hemmed in by restrictions and limitations.
11. Some of your aspirations tend to be pretty unrealistic.
12. You have a great deal of unused capacity which you have not turned to your advantage.

The other problem is remembering all these lines. There are only twelve, but the concepts aren't very 'sticky', they don't seem to be 'about' anything, and there is a tendency to remember only a couple of them and forget the rest as at first glance they appear quite similar.

However, if you can remember all these lines and apply the concepts of each line to a person in a useful and interesting way, you have something incredibly powerful at your disposal - the ability to appear to know an awful lot about someone with no previous information. Before we discuss the application of these lines however we must first commit them to memory, and this is where James Bond comes into it.

Before I explain the James Bond Cold Reading to you, I want you to imagine that James Bond is standing in front of you, and you're going to tell him about himself. Unlike any stranger you may meet, you know a lot about James Bond already! Off the top of your head you could probably say:

- **You like the attention of the opposite sex, when it suits you**
- **Sometimes you feel as if you are leading a double life**
- **You've had your fair share of exciting times in the past**
- **You like to look your best but sometimes that can be difficult**
- **You have to look out for yourself much of the time and be careful who you trust**
- **There was someone a while back who you sometimes wonder you should have settled down with**

I could go on, and these were literally off the top of my head. But can you start to see what I am getting at? By basing my suppositions on a character I already know, I am coming up with some of my own truisms myself, similar in many ways to the twelve lines of the classic reading. I'm sure that most of these last points probably apply to you as much as me. However, I was simply imagining what it must be like to be in James Bond's shoes and coming up with concepts that I thought pertained to him.

So having a character in mind can be inspirational, and because I'm actually thinking about a person, although fictional, my ideas are useful and valid and could apply to almost anyone. What's great about thinking about larger than life characters such as James Bond is that they conjure up many images, feelings and ideas and as they are fictional, they are fully rounded (unlike real people, who sometimes tend not to be!)

To take this idea a step further, we can write a new version of the Classic Reading, substituting lines as they may pertain to James Bond for the original lines. These lines do not replace the Classic Reading lines entirely, moreover they help us remember each one by association with the James Bond character.

In order to help continuity and memorization we can also try and link each line into a sequence where one line follows on to the next. By chaining the lines and concepts into a plot, we can quickly learn the twelve steps as if we were in James Bond's shoes, which in turn means we can remember each of the Classic Reading lines extremely quickly.

The James Bond Cold Reading

1. **You are planning your mission alone, before socializing at the swanky party.**
2. **You are centre of attention at the party, which you enjoy.**
3. **Although cool and confident, you are nervous about the mission.**
4. **And as a perfectionist, you hope this mission goes to plan.**
5. **Although you have intelligence about Dr No, you need to find the real truth.**
6. **You cannot be too open or it would give your identity away.**
7. **Your sexual side has caused its fair share of problems.**
8. **Although you have your vices, you are able to compensate in other ways.**
9. **At times you wonder if being a spy was the correct path for you.**
10. **You prefer change and variety though so it suits you.**
11. **Some of your plot-lines tend to be pretty unrealistic.**
12. **Even so, you still have some surprises left in you.**

As you can see, the James Bond lines are actually simpler than the Classic Reading lines, although they do contain the seed of what you need to elaborate on each idea. It is remembering these ideas which is more important than learning each Classic Reading line accurately, and I know from personal experience that my first stumbling block was trying to learn each line of the Classic Reading 'word perfect' before I went on.

YOU DO NOT NEED TO REMEMBER EACH LINE OF THE CLASSIC READING WORD PERFECT!
What is important is that you remember the *concept* of each line, so you can
speak about them in your own words, depending on the situation

On the next few pages I will go through each step and elaborate on what you *could* say. People who know my other books (such as Palm Reading In Your Own Words) know I am a great believer in finding your own voice. You need to make these ideas work for YOU and not be a slave to them. Grab the key concepts about each line, and then elaborate on them in your own words. This is when these ideas are their most valuable. Practice seeing how many ways you could extemporize on a line. Speak to the walls, or practice recording your own voice. Put yourself on the spot before someone else does! It's amazing how much confidence you can gain by simply trying to give inanimate objects a reading!

Read the 'You could say..' sections only as a guide to get your own ideas flowing. As practice, read each line of the James Bond Classic Reading and then try and come up with ten DIFFERENT things you could say based on each line. These 'You could say..' ideas are not perfect by any stretch of the imagination, but they are short and to the point. When you come up with lines yourself on the spur of the moment, they should be a springboard to engaging the person you are reading. The aim is to create a two way dialogue if possible.

If you are trying to learn the 'You could say..' sections then you are missing the whole idea - so don't let me catch you doing it!

The James Bond Script

The twelve steps of the James Bond Script

---

1   You are planning your mission alone, before socializing at the swanky party.

o   (Classic: At times you are extroverted, affable, sociable, while at other times you are introverted, wary, and reserved.)

James Bond always lives this double-life where he spends a lot of time alone quietly planning his next move, before going out there and mingling with the in-crowd. Most people need solitude and socializing in regular doses.

You could say:

- Sometimes you like to scheme alone and not let people into your private world, but after a while this can become too much and you like to let your hair down and mingle.
- You are sociable, but like private time to do your own thing.
- You have an independent streak which others can see in you, but you don't let it get in the way of family and friends.
- Although people think you have a tendency to jump into things, secretly you are a little more reserved than that and do give things more thought than people would give you credit for.
- There is always a need for you to charge your batteries and have some 'me' time, although you can have fun when you want to.
- You know when to stop when it's good for you.
- Some people don't think you have a plan, but you do, of sorts, even though it may not fit in with their own plans!

The James Bond Script

The twelve steps of the James Bond Script

---

2   You are the centre of attention at the party, which you enjoy.

    o   (Classic: You have a strong need for other people to like you and for them to admire you.)

James Bond loves the attention and admiration, even though it can be his undoing sometimes. Most people are like this, even the quietest people like attention.

You could say:

- Sometimes you feel under-appreciated and feel that people don't understand how hard you try
- Even though you can be shy, you do like to be the centre of attention
- Some people think you're an attention seeker but in actual fact you just want to be noticed
- You are proud of your achievements but unfortunately this can rub some people up the wrong way
- You're a people person in as much as you like to be needed, and some respect wouldn't go amiss either!
- You enjoy other people's company when it's right for you
- Although you are humble in many ways, you do feel that people to look up to you sometimes

The James Bond Script

The twelve steps of the James Bond Script

---

3   Although cool and confident, you are nervous about the mission.

> o   (Classic: Disciplined and controlled on the outside, you tend to be worrisome and insecure on the inside.)

James Bond is the king of bravado. His steely exterior belies the complex and emotional nature he must keep to himself in order to succeed. He is only human after all.

You could say:

- To many people you do things effortlessly, although you have your own worries
- Sometimes you find it hard to let your guard down and let people see your own insecurities
- You have learnt that in order to succeed you must often keep yourself to yourself
- Showing your true emotions has sometimes been a problem for you as you try and be there for everyone else
- You have an inner determination that can keep you going no matter how tough things appear
- Friends see you as a shoulder to cry on although sometimes you'd like to borrow theirs!
- You've had to keep your feelings to yourself sometimes so as not to upset other people

The James Bond Script

The twelve steps of the James Bond Script

---

4   And as a perfectionist, you hope this mission goes to plan.

      o   (Classic: You have a tendency to be critical of yourself.)

James Bond is his own harshest critic. He demands a lot from himself. Just like we all do of ourselves, sometimes with tough consequences.

You could say:

- You can often be your worst critic, and can often hear praise as putdown
- You like things to be just-so and this has caused some friction in your life
- You always hope for the best but secretly always try to be better
- You sometimes worry about where you are going and blame yourself too much for the way your life has gone
- Even when you achieve great things you rarely give yourself the credit you deserve
- You shouldn't expect everyone to be able to live up to the demands you make from yourself
- You are a perfectionist, even if to some people it doesn't come across like that

The James Bond Script

The twelve steps of the James Bond Script

---

5   Although you have intelligence about Dr No, you need to find the real truth.

    o   (Classic: You pride yourself on being an independent thinker and do not accept others' opinions without satisfactory proof.)

The James Bond films are all about what James discovers during the unfolding story. Starting with little information he finds his own way and the real truth behind the plot-line. His independence is the key to finding the facts.

You could say:

- Although you can be a good listener you like to make your own mind up about things
- Knowing what's really going on is important to you, but sometimes this can land you in trouble
- You've always had a longing and a searching for your own truth
- You are not easily swayed and can make your own decisions
- You can be quite stubborn at times and often take a lot of convincing
- Sometimes your sense of pride can get in the way of clear thinking
- You like to mull over the finer details before coming to conclusions, however this does not mean you are slow to act when you think you are right

The James Bond Script

The twelve steps of the James Bond Script

---

6   You cannot be too open or it would give your identity away.

   o   (Classic: You have found it unwise to be too frank in revealing yourself to others.)

If James Bond was too open about who he was he wouldn't get very far. However, when the time is right he knows when to open up.

You could say:

- Although you are quite an open person, you have learnt to be cautious
- You have learnt through experience that you can't trust everybody and it isn't always wise to wear your heart on your sleeve
- Sometimes you've 'let people in' too soon and have later regretted it
- Although you're a naturally strong willed person, you can tend to wonder who you really are
- There is a lot going on underneath the surface with you, and only people that you've really got to know will ever see that side of you
- Some people think they really know you when they've barely scratched the surface and this can leave you feeling a little lonely
- Like most people you've had your fair share of knocks and because of this you choose your friends carefully before divulging your innermost thoughts and fears

The James Bond Script

The twelve steps of the James Bond Script

---

7   Your sexual side has caused its fair share of problems.

> o   (Classic: Your sexual adjustment has presented some problems for you.)

Wouldn't you say that James Bond's sexual nature hasn't got him into some difficult situations?

You could say:

- Sometimes you've found members of the opposite sex to be a real mystery
- Matters of the heart have challenged and perplexed you in the past, however I feel you are coming to a new level of understanding about life, love and the opposite sex
- I see a time when you didn't quite feel comfortable with your sexuality and who you are, but as you've grown you've learnt to love yourself and others in your own way
- Some of the confusion of your teenage years with boyfriends/girlfriends is still with you and sometimes you still feel like you're not sure what you're doing
- Although you're quite a passionate person sometimes you can find it difficult to express it emotionally
- Your love life has often confused you and created conflicting emotions
- Your need to be wanted and loved has sometimes attracted the wrong kind of person in your life

The James Bond Script

The twelve steps of the James Bond Script

---

8 Although you have your vices, you are able to compensate in other ways.

o (Classic: While you have some personality weaknesses, you are generally able to compensate for them.)

James Bond has enough vices to clamp the whole of Western Europe. But we love him for it, as he more than makes up for it in other ways and shows that he is human.

You could say:

- You can be rather hasty with some things that you find annoying, however you can spend hours doing things you really love
- You know you're not perfect but feel that you make up for this in other ways that some people don't appreciate
- You know what you like and can be compulsive sometimes but this doesn't mean you don't have restraint, you are just picky about when to use it
- You do a lot of good in your life although you do worry about even the smallest imperfections
- Giving yourself a hard time about things can waste a lot of time, even though you know that you more than make up for your shortcomings
- There are things you wish you could be better and more talented at and this sometimes prevents you seeing the good you do in other areas
- Nobody's perfect and you would be the first to agree about that even though sometimes you can find it hard to admit your own imperfections

The James Bond Script

The twelve steps of the James Bond Script

---

9   At times you wonder if being a spy was the correct path for you.

> o   (Classic: At times you have serious doubts as to whether you have made the right decision or done the right thing.)

James Bond often has doubts about his chosen career path and is often confronted with conflicting choices. This is the humanity which makes him so endearing as a character.

You could say:

- You have a tendency to reflect on the past a little too much sometimes
- Making choices can be a cause of concern for you as you know that in the past you haven't always made the best of choices
- You shouldn't worry too much about the paths you have taken in your life, they all happen for a reason and are leading you to quite a good place
- If you were to worry less about so of the more dubious decisions you have made up to know, you could enjoy the present a lot more
- The grass is always greener on the other side and sometimes you wonder what it may be like to be in someone else's shoes
- You can tend to be a bit worrisome and the past can trouble you sometimes
- You can't change the past so you should stop worrying about it and move into the future happy and confident that all things have led to the present moment

The James Bond Script

The twelve steps of the James Bond Script

---

10 You prefer change and variety though so it suits you.

 o (Classic: You prefer a certain amount of change and variety and become dissatisfied when hemmed in by restrictions and limitations.)

James Bond obviously prefers change and variety and hates being told what to do, even on an important mission! He has defied his orders many times but been proven right just as many...

You could say:

- You like your home comforts but a little excitement now and again wouldn't go amiss
- You've always been unconventional, and sometimes not in ways that anyone would notice readily
- Freedom is important to you and you don't always feel comfortable being told what to do
- Although you know when to hold your cool, you have sometimes thought of yourself as a quite rebel
- Being able to do what you want when you want is important to you, although life sometimes just doesn't comply
- You may have noticed that when you become miserable or disheartened it's often because you feel trapped in some way, and this may go back to feelings you had when you were younger
- Sometimes you've had to secretly go against what other people may see as right or wrong, simply to ensure that people don't get hurt

The James Bond Script

The twelve steps of the James Bond Script

---

11 Some of your plot-lines tend to be pretty unrealistic.

  o   (Classic: Some of your aspirations tend to be pretty unrealistic.)

Of course, the Bond films and books have some of the most unrealistic and fantastical plot-lines going. People who want to be like James Bond are also having ideas above their station!

You could say:

- You have a tendency to fantasize somewhat about what may happen in your life
- You're not a typical dreamer, although you've done your fair share of wishful thinking
- Sometimes the realities of everyday life can bore you and you can find yourself hoping for some magic wand to change the way things are
- You can be quite stubborn and find it difficult to admit when you've had ideas above your station
- You've learnt the hard way that sometimes trying to be what you're not can be painful, however you keep on trying and that's a good thing
- When you're trying so hard to be good at things you think you should be good at, you can forget how good you are at things you already know
- Even though you will achieve a lot of your dreams and goals, you're going to have to learn to prioritize those that are most important to you

The James Bond Script

The twelve steps of the James Bond Script

---

12 Even so, you still have some surprises left in you.

    o   (Classic: You have a great deal of unused capacity which you have not turned to your advantage.)

James Bond ALWAYS has a surprise left in store, even when he's in the tightest corner. Most people have hidden abilities which they have not drawn upon in their lives.

You could say:

- You are yet to fully capitalize on all of your talents, some which have laid dormant for many years
- I feel that you have many abilities that have been hiding until the time is right
- Although you're quite a giving person, you would probably have more to give if you were able to unlock some of your hidden potential
- Sometimes you are so busy thinking about the here and now that you forget just how resourceful you can be
- You don't need to look outward for anything that you need as you have everything right there inside you, even though some of it seems locked away or hard to get at
- It can be frustrating when you have so many ideas and hard to focus on any one of them
- You can be a source of frustration to your friends who can see your potential even though most of the time you are blissfully unaware of it

The James Bond Plot

We have the script lines, but to properly remember all of them we need to string them together with a visualization or 'plot'. By thinking between the lines of the script, we can join up each script line so that each leads into the next.

To do this we go through the script lines one by one and create a strong mental picture of each and use these to create a whole scene. This can be enhanced by adding movement and actions to the unfolding 'story' to aid visualization.

Here is the plot I use - feel free to create your own should you wish. It doesn't matter what you come up with as long as you can remember it- no one else will know how you string the script lines together.

Script line	**Plot**
1. You are planning your mission alone, before socializing at the swanky party.	You are in your hotel room going through your mission documents which are contained in your hi-tech briefcase, planning your mission alone before locking up the secrets safely and hiding the briefcase under the bed. You then put your jacket on and take a quick look in the mirror before taking the stairs down to the drinks reception.
2. You are centre of attention at the party, which you enjoy.	You are quickly surrounded by your acquaintances and admirers and are soon able to shake of the thoughts of your mission a little and relax into the mood of the evening. As always you are comfortable and relaxed in this environment.
3. Although cool and confident, you are nervous about the mission.	You can't totally shake off the thoughts of the mission however, the memories of the documents and what you have to achieve are never far from your mind. Some people eye you suspiciously from across the room making you feel a little uneasy.
4. And as a perfectionist, you hope this mission goes to plan.	Like all your missions there is no margin for error. Only by being meticulous can you ensure that everything goes to plan. You brush off a small piece of fluff from your collar and adjust your tie.

5. Although you have intelligence about Dr No, you need to find the real truth.

Getting your wallet out of your jacket pocket, you open it and take a quick look at a photograph of Dr No to refresh your memory. You've been told he runs this hotel from a secret basement, but you need to find out for yourself.

6. You cannot be too open or it would give your identity away.

A young lady strolls over to you from across the room. You quickly hide the photo and put the wallet back in your pocket. One slip of your true identity would be a mistake at this point.

7. Your sexual side has caused its fair share of problems.

She is quite attractive and you wonder if she is some kind of bait. You've had problems with women in the past. She asks for a light for her cigarette.

8. Although you have your vices, you are able to compensate in other ways.

You light her cigarette, but instead of taking one from her, you pull out a nicotine chewing gum and start chewing on it. You have been trying to kick the habit for years but it's always been difficult to avoid it.

9. At times you wonder if being a spy was the correct path for you.

The lady walks off and you pause to reflect on the past, the adventures, the excitement. Perhaps you should have settled down with a nice lady like that you wonder.

10. You prefer change and variety though so it suits you.

No sooner have you thought that an absolute stunning leggy blonde who must be without a doubt your next 'Bond Girl' walks into the room to the turning of heads.

11. Some of your plot-lines tend to be pretty un-realistic.

The 'Bond Girl' walks over to you and introduces you to her entourage of ninja-dwarves who are breeding a super-race of man eating guinea pigs in a desperate bid to conquer the universe.

12. Even so, you still have some surprises left in you.

However, you reach into your back pocket and bring out some 'Ninja-Be-Gone' spray and within a few seconds you have banished the entire lot.

Don't forget, if you're not happy doing it in the third person (as in 'watching' James Bond) then you could always do it in first person and imagine YOU are James Bond! Do whatever you find easiest.

USE THE FLASH CARDS!

The flash cards that accompany this book are an extremely useful study tool. Print them out and use them!

Each card has one of The James Bond Cold Reading script lines on the front, with it's Classic Reading equivalent in smaller print.

On the back of each card is the plot visualization to help you remember the whole script.

There is space on the front of each card to write your own notes and add your own ideas.

See how quickly you can learn all twelve lines!

Retention

Here's a brief summary on how we're going to remember all this:

- We have twelve classic reading lines
- To help us remember the concepts of the classic reading lines, we have twelve script lines
- Each script line revolves around the James Bond character
- To remember the script lines we create a plot that links each line together

Therefore when we want to recall the twelve classic reading line concepts:

- The plot will help us remember the script lines
- The script lines will help us remember the classic reading concepts

When you first start learning this, imagine yourself as a 'fly on the wall' in James Bond's life. Imagine him planning his mission in his hotel room before walking down the stairs to the casino drinks party, imagine him being the centre of attention with people taking an interest, imagine him trying to maintain this facade even though he's wondering if he can pull the whole thing off...

By visualizing like this you will have quite an elaborate scene built up by the end of the twelfth step. Make it your own, create your own world with these twelve steps, and you will never be short of something to say in a reading again.

As with most memory work, I have made some parts of the plot quite silly in a bid to conjure up stronger images that can be remembered more easily. The main idea here is to create moments that lead to other moments enabling you to remember the entire plot as a chain of events.

Another aid to remembering the plot is to cut it into two sections. Try remembering the whole thing, but then try doing it from step 7 onwards from when you give the girl a light. Also try remembering it in reverse order - all these things help implant the sequence in your mind.

Here's what we need to do to learn the lines as quickly as possible:

- Read through the Classic Reading lines a few times to make yourself familiar with them (page 8)
- Read through the James Bond Classic Reading a few times and get a feel for how these can be linked together (page 10)
- Read through the James Bond Script Lines and see how each script line corresponds with each Classic Reading line (page 11)
- Run through The Plot a few times, visualizing each step as you go (page 23)
- Use the flash cards to help you do this

To practice:

- Try and remember the plot, starting from James Bond in his hotel room
- As you remember the plot, try and remember each script line
- As you remember each script line, remember each classic reading concept and say something out loud that echoes that concept (yes, out loud, in your own words!)
- See if you can get through all twelve lines

Sometimes you will make it through the plot but will find you've missed a couple of bits out. Just count how many you've managed to recall and simply go back and find the lines you missed, and strengthen the visualization at those points.

You will find that plot and line eventually become tied together and you will be remembering the ideas all in one go - sometimes the script line will remind you of the scene, sometimes the Classic Reading line will remind you of the plot! It doesn't matter - what does matter is that you remember it all.

As always the emphasis is on recalling the ideas behind the classic lines and not the lines themselves. When you first recall James Bond getting ready for the party in his hotel room alone, you will be reminded that he likes time alone and socializing in equal amounts. As soon as you have remembered that, SAY SOMETHING ABOUT IT. Don't think too hard, learn to speak out loud and off the cuff about the concept. You can see from the script section some of my own 'You could say..' ideas which I've come up with, but you need to practice creating your own. IMMEDIATELY.

As you have learned the concepts of each line instead of each of them in parrot fashion, you have a certain amount of freedom to express these ideas. However you do need to PRACTICE. With these twelve truisms at your disposal you are never going to be wrong, so you should at least be confident that no matter what you come out with based on each idea, the worst that could happen is that you come across a bit vague!

(If you print this ebook out you will find there is plenty of space left underneath my own ideas in The James Bond Script section for you to write your own. This was intentional.)

The main reason many stock lines fail to be put into practice is not only that they are difficult to remember, but the student feels they need to learn each line by rote. This is absurd, as reeling off the Classic Reading lines one by one is an incredibly unnatural thing to do. By vaguely remembering the concept of each line and putting those ideas into your own words you will come across as an empathic individual who really does seem to be connecting with someone using a certain amount of effort, skill and judgement. Your struggle to find words will make you sweat, and as everyone wants to think of themselves as a completely unique individual, your difficulty and then subsequent success will make people feel not only that they are special, but that your talents are real and hard learned.

SECTION TWO

Application

Cold Reading As Effect

Application

Many books and manuscripts with stock lines in their pages say very little about using this information in any useful way. By learning the twelve classic reading lines, you have twelve concepts that you can elaborate on at a moments notice. But let's not forget that you actually have to express this to someone - the person you are 'reading'.

You could be reading someone's palm, and then decide to throw in one of the classic reading ideas to add a little spice. But I think the best way to practice using these lines is to do something bold and simply tell people about themselves, based on what they're like! There is something quite liberating about 'going for it'.

Before you start ANY kind of reading however, there are two simple things you can do to create an open dialogue between you and your 'spectator'.

Diffuse any idea that the reading is a challenge

By asking for help, openness and honesty to ensure the success of the reading, the thought that this may be a challenge never enters the spectator's mind. Emphasis is placed firmly on the idea that the reading is a two-way process.

Share responsibility for the reading with the spectator

No one wants to be a failure. By hinting that the reading will only work with successful cooperation primes the spectator to be helpful. Like all people, they want to be told nice things about themselves, and if it is made clear that their cooperation is essential for this to happen they will be all the more willing.

The key words here really are 'open dialogue'. A reading is a two way street, and by letting the spectator know that the reading is a joint effort opens the whole process up. All ideas that the reading is a challenge evaporate when you do this. The reading is a process, not an outcome.

With this in mind, and with only a few Classic Reading lines at your disposal, you can get quite a lot of mileage if you use a chatty approach and you can get the other person talking. The key is to tie in what you're saying with some obvious visual cue or personality trait that everyone can see.

Backtrack the reading into the purported method

By referring your words back to your supposed method, your reading will be legitimized and your method will be believed.

For example, if you were reading someone's palm and you came out with 'Although people think you have a tendency to jump into things, secretly you are a little more reserved than that and do give things more thought than people would give you credit for' then they'd quite often ask you which part of their palm gave you that information. By referencing parts of the palm as the basic source of the information the ideas are legitimized, as with all forms of divination.

But you don't have to do this just with palms, why not simply say 'I've been looking at your clothes and how you hold your posture and I'd say you were quite happy go lucky on the outside and most people think you're always fun and out there. Looking at your handbag, however, which is quite a simple design and your shoes which although very pretty aren't anything as wild as the fun I've seen you have tonight, I get the feeling that you are far more reserved than people give you credit for and can actually be a bit of a worrier sometimes.' In a casual setting this kind of thing can quickly get people interested in your 'abilities' and before long, you guessed it, most people will be asking if you can read palms and you will have grabbed all their friends to 'be read' via any means you happen to have at your disposal. By linking your thoughts to some kind of 'system' makes the whole thing far more believable, especially when you're starting out, even if the system you are referring to is being made up on the spot!

Of course, you could go through the entire list of the classic reading with one person, but then if this is the only 'system' you have learned you are going to be short of things to say to other people who may also be present. Of course in one on one readings this doesn't really matter, but in a more social setting it can be a problem. My advice is to use a few lines on each person in this situation.

As you now know, no one knows you're thinking of James Bond at all. However, as soon as you want to tell someone about themselves, you simply remember James Bond in his hotel room pouring over his secret documents before he goes and socializes (Step 1). This in turn reminds you that most people enjoy solitude and socializing in equal amounts. Then your mouth engages and you come out with something like 'I get the sense that sometimes you like to scheme alone and not let people into your private world, but after a while this can become too much and you like to let your hair down and mingle.'

After this you then remember Step 2, about being the center of attention at the party. Then you say something about that. And you can keep going like this through each step until you've had enough, or the 'reading' has gone off somewhere entirely independent of your stock lines. But it's a good feeling knowing you've ALWAYS got something to say whenever you need it and can go on at quite some length.

And you don't have to start at step 1. You can pick the lines out pretty randomly once you're familiar with the story. Why not start at step 7 or 8 and then jump to step 2? You could use the first three lines on one person in a group, the next three on a second person and another three lines on a third person. If you're really good at this stuff you can probably milk enough out of each line for one person one line.

Something else which needs to be addressed is the fact that you're not just talking to a wall, you are talking to a human being. Let the other person react to what you're saying by talking slowly, and leaving gaps, sometimes quite big ones, between the ideas and lines you are coming out with. If you pause, the person you are reading (or their friends in a social surrounding) will be inclined to fill in the gaps. Silence can work for you so use it! The silence doesn't only have to be broken by the person you are reading, quite often their friends will help out by agreeing with you or saying something, or until they're told to be quiet at least, which is always amusing.

Whenever you get agreement with some kind of information (and it will be fairly often with the classic reading) you should continue as if you knew all along which information was relevant. For example, if you say something like 'You tend to dwell on the past a little too much sometimes' and the person responds by divulging some information regarding a previous relationship they have yet to get over, you could add 'Yes and I also get the feeling that you've been finding it hard to come to terms with being alone again.' By appearing to continue your train of thought after they have divulged this information makes it seem as if you knew about the relationship all along and their input was in fact agreeing with you. Of course this is not the case, but without pauses to let the person try to make sense of your classic reading lines you are not going to be able to elaborate on them.

Something else you should do is create a positive projection about the future of these developments or ideas. So as with our last example you could then say 'I can see by your determination and strong attitude that you are now coming to a new period in your life where you are able to let go of those things that have been holding you back and start a new chapter. Although sometimes you may feel that a cloud has yet to lift, you are very close to being back on track and with just a bit more perseverance which it is obvious that you have, you can look forward to a brighter future and I can definitely see someone special entering your life.'

Now that may seem like quite a lot, but what have a really said? All I have done in effect is be really 'nice'. I've just been really positive about her future relationship prospects and her ability to get over the past, simply because she told me that that was where the problems lie. You know that you are probably going to get a 'hit' with each of these lines, but by letting the person tell you exactly which part of their lives you have connected with you are in a position to elaborate on this in a positive way. The original classic reading line will be forgotten and all that will be remembered is that you told someone that they will soon get over their previous relationship problems and in the future you see things turning out better for them. And because you already 'knew' about their relationship problems in the first place (apparently) your positive future projection will be believed.

Of course, you need to temper this with some kind of realism. Painting a rosy picture every single time will come across as insincere gushing drivel which you need to avoid! Try and keep it real by adding 'warnings' based on what you have just said. These are basically things to look out for, and can be arrived at by simply using your common sense. Again taking the lead from the previous example you could say 'One thing I do know is that you're going to be a lot more careful in the near future and are going to spend a lot more effort looking after number one. Be careful that you haven't closed up too much for other people to get through your new barriers as this can scare a lot of people off. However you've learned a few lessons over the last year or two and you've grown up in many ways, so you are far less likely to suffer fools gladly.'

As you can see, I've simply elaborated even further on what has gone before in the form of some 'advice'. As a reader I don't really recommend giving advice out to people, but by being careful with your words you can appear to give advice when in fact all you're stating is the obvious. Of course this person is going to be a lot more careful, she's just getting over a relationship! And of course, she's going to be wary, and is probably worried of being too tough on her next suitor. It is all completely obvious, but you need to state the obvious as if it were revelatory.

Don't forget that when you are talking in vague terms, the person who is listening to you is connecting what you are saying to her own HARD FACTS. If you can find out what you have connected with, you can then take credit for being incredibly wise and intuitive by elaborating on her facts instead of your initial idea. It will be believed that you knew the hard facts all along.

In this rambling example I have said a lot to this lady, all from one line. These lines are springboards to get the reading going and that's how they should be used. Please believe me when I say that NO ONE ever thought that by simply reciting these twelve lines at someone that you would be able to make an impression - you still need to think on your feet and extemporize. With the twelve lines under your belt however you have twelve sure-fire ways of starting a train of thought which can lead in new directions.

Of course, sometimes when you give a reading you are going to get absolutely no response from the person at all. In fact, this can happen quite often. If your pauses and quizzical looks are failing to get responses then I'm afraid you have to go with your feelings and elaborate slightly more vaguely. What you will find though is that after a while you will have hit something that the person connects with more than others and the person will find it hard not to give you some kind of reaction. In these situations you just have to work with what you're got. But as you've got the twelve lines, you're hardly going to be wrong anyway.

When the response is less than great however, you can do one of two things

Either

Gloss over the negative response from the spectator entirely and go straight into another classic reading concept

This is fairly easy, just keep talking and move on to the next Classic Reading concept! It's as if you were trying to work something out, but this train of thought led you to the next stage. So you weren't wrong, you were thinking out loud.

Or

Re-frame the previous concept as if the spectator had misinterpreted what you meant

The spectator looks at you as if your last statement was wrong. Re-phrase your last statement in a different light to explain what you 'really meant'. Even simpler, pick one key phrase from your 'wrong' statement that the spectator couldn't possibly disagree with and elaborate on that, ignoring everything else you said.

TO RECAP:
- Come out with your ideas slowly with lots of gaps between them
- Link the ideas to some external thing or method where possible
- When you get some kind of response LET THEM SPEAK
- Use their input as part of your longer sentence
- Develop these ideas into the future with a positive outcome
- Temper your positive projections with warnings based on common sense

This is something you should practice. Try each classic reading idea on an imaginary person and think about what they might say, and react accordingly.

Cold Reading As Effect

'Cold Reading' is a catch-all phrase for a whole variety of techniques, the twelve lines of the Classic Reading being just one of the ways in which we can start the reading process. However, it is up to the performer to decide when and where to use Cold Reading and to what aim.

For explanatory purposes during this section I am going to assume that we are presenting ourselves as non-psychic entertainers who use 'scientific' methods to glean our information.

Many effects need to be substantially re-worked to incorporate a Cold Reading that is going to be effective. You need only the simplest of excuses to deliver an effective Cold Reading however. Even the oldest trick in the book, 'pick a card', can be re-worked to incorporate a reading.

Let us talk about when it WON'T work first though.

Imagine you pick a random card from a normal deck of cards without showing me. I want to tell you about the card and 'throw in' some cold reading. But I can't! You just picked the card at random, I've got nothing to 'hang' my cold reading on. Even if I knew which card you picked, it wouldn't tell me anything about you. It was random. Your personality didn't get involved.

To change the effect to incorporate Cold Reading your personal input must be included so at least I can show that there was some way I could have known what you may have chosen, by backtracking through your choices taking your personality into account, thereby 'concluding' that you must have picked such and such a card.

To allow cold reading to become part of your mentalism effects you need to open them up so that cold reading can be allowed in. By this I mean you need to put the choices firmly in the minds of your spectator, just as you would with a more traditional reading. The spectator needs to have thought carefully about the numbers they have picked, the colours they have marked or the words they have written. The things they commit to memory or paper must be as personal to them as possible. There must be talk of choices, decisions, consequences and personal actions. By conversing in these terms you are setting yourself up so that you can always attribute your knowledge of what someone wrote, scribbled or thought of to your ability to 'read' people, be it by cod-psychology, intuition or whatever.

By changing the pick a card effect slightly, we can appear to give ourselves something to 'read'. For example, I scatter the pack of 52 cards in front of you face up, turn my back, and tell you to think very carefully about which card you are going to choose. When you have taken a card I turn around, and by assessing your clothes, posture and demeanor I finally arrive at the card you chose. Because I gave you a free choice of card, I can make it appear that I arrived at your choice through a mixture of subconscious cues that I picked up from you and therefore backtrack to your choice. Of course I knew the card you picked because I cheated in some way, but nevertheless I made you believe that my ability to know what kind of person you are led me to your card. I am so clever!

BUT WAIT. This effect may still not be cold reading. If all I've done is looked you up and down, scratched my chin a few times and said 'Ace Of Spades' then this isn't cold reading at all. To make it a cold reading I really have to tell you things about yourself that I couldn't possibly know - I have to prove beyond doubt that my intuition goes further than just being able to see that you chose the Ace Of Spades because you like heavy metal. Many mentalists confuse this post-justification process for cold reading. Saying something like '...and I can tell because of your long hair and your nose stud you probably like rock music so you chose the Ace Of Spades' isn't really cold reading. It's more like post-justification.

By using cold reading techniques you should be able to take a pick a card routine much further. By the end of it you should have come across as someone who 'knows', not someone who takes random stabs in the dark and looks like they probably cheated anyway.

Here is our humble pick-a-card trick scripted out as it may happen using the concepts of the twelve classic reading lines. To save time with the explanation, let me just tell you that the cards are stacked beforehand and that's all the preparation you need. As it's quite difficult to create a living and talking spectator on the page, let's just imagine that our imaginary spectator called Pam isn't particularly responsive to our host, Chris Reader.

Chris Reader uses all twelve classic reading concepts, in order, through this routine. See if you can spot them!

Chris Reader: Hi my name's Chris Reader and I'd like to try a little experiment with you if I may. I've got a pack of cards here and as you can see like all packs we have the spades, hearts, diamonds and clubs, as well as the numbers one to ten and the face cards Jack, Queen and King. I'm going to hand you the pack, and if you could I would like you to keep cutting the pack over and over again like this, ok?

(performer hands cards to Pam)

While you're doing that I'd like you to think of all the numbers in your life that have a special significance for you, the colours that surround you every day, and the faces that make you happy. As you keep cutting the cards, let your mind drift and in doing so, allow your thoughts to settle on a card that you think might have some significance for you. Don't rush this, it may take some time for a card to reveal itself to you, but please, keep it to yourself, I don't want to know what it is just yet.

When you have settled on a card please stop cutting the cards and place the pack back on the table face down. I will turn my back before you do this so please let me know when you have finished but do take as long as you like. I need you to choose the card and the card to choose you, so please take your time.

(The performer turns away from Pam. Pam finally thinks of a card, and puts the cards face down onto the table.)

Pam: OK, I've done that.

Chris Reader: You've finished? Good. Now just so that everyone else here can know what card it is you're thinking of too, and so I don't overhear anything, can you just turn cards face up one at a time into another pile and stop when you get to your card? Thanks, and when you do come to the card you were thinking of can you please show it to everyone here and then put it in your pocket so there's no way I could see it. Tell me when you've done that. Good, and can someone else collect up the cards so that no cards are to be seen anywhere? Thanks, let me know when all the cards are put away and I'll turn back round.

(Note: Chris turns around slightly just after the thought of card has been placed in the pocket as he remarks about having the rest of the cards put away. In that moment he peeks the face up card on the table, which immediately tells him which card Pam is thinking of due to the stack. This ruse of turning around to take a peek at something goes back to Annemann.)

Pam: Done it!

(The performer turns to face Pam)

So Pam, I don't know much about you so to help me do this I am going to need you to be fairly open and honest with me, ok? If we could just talk about you a little bit that would be great. Now I've noticed that you didn't take much prompting to take part in this experiment so I think I would be right in saying that you're quite an outgoing type of person. What I'm noticing already however is that being put on the spot like this isn't entirely natural for you is it? I think you're the kind of person who enjoys these kinds of get-togethers but you also like your home comforts and could just as happily sit at home with your feet up. Even though secretly you can be a little shy, you do like being the centre of attention as you are now, don't you?

Pam: (laughs) Yes.

Chris: Have you always been like that?

Pam: Kind of.

Chris Reader: I get the feeling that this could have been like some kind of defense mechanism perhaps, and as you grew up you felt a need to assert yourself, but the shyness never left you totally. I get a sense that you still get a little nervous around certain people but you've learned to bottle it up and in fact 'being loud' has helped you in life. You're certainly a colourful character, and I'd hazard a guess that you thought of a red card, is that correct?

Pam: Yes.

Chris Reader: Ok we're getting somewhere now, I'm starting to build a picture up in my mind. I'd say from looking at your immaculate appearance you can tend to be overly critical of yourself, it must take a lot of effort to look that good! There have probably been issues in the past with people being jealous of you, but that's unfair as they don't know what you've been through. Being critical of yourself however can sometimes mean you're rather critical of others, even though most of the time you don't let on, other people can be rather disappointing sometimes! Would that be a fair assumption?

Pam: Yeah, well..

Chris Reader: But you have been let down in the past haven't you?

Pam: Yeah..

Chris Reader: You see, you can be quite headstrong and this one of your strengths. You like to know what's what on your own terms, and you don't just believe what everyone is telling you - you like to find things out for yourself. But because of these let downs you've learned to keep things to yourself a lot more, wouldn't you say?

Pam: Uh-uh, I guess I know when to shut up (laughs)

Chris Reader: Yes, and this is why this is proving quite difficult? You're really not giving too much away. In fact it's not so much about what you're saying, it's about what you're not saying! But I think because of this you didn't pick a people card like a Jack, Queen or King did you, you chose a number card I think, is that correct? Yes I thought to, you see, you are a people person to most people, but there's an awful lot going on under the bonnet than most people would give you credit for.

Now I would imagine that this has presented all kind of challenges for you, but you do seem to have a heart of gold, I can really feel that and I know I'm not alone in that sense, I'm sure that everyone here can feel that. I mean along with the being critical of yourself you know you do have faults, but you are able to compensate for them in other ways, wouldn't you say?

Pam: Yeah sure, we all have our problems..

Chris Reader: But wouldn't you say that in many ways this drives you forward? I see you as a problem solver, you are able to see quite clearly what you are like and move on, almost using your shortcomings as fuel to do good things for yourself and others. We all have our faults, but I think you have a unique way of dealing with yours in the way you can turn them to your advantage. It's this kind of thinking that also made me think you chose a number card. But also the fact that you have this soft almost nurturing side makes me think you probably settled on a heart, is that correct?

Pam: Yes!

Chris Reader: Ok, so for some reason your personality talked to you and whispered a heart shaped number card to you. Now this could be a low number, a middle number or a high number. No don't smile too much, I don't want too many clues!

Pam: (laughs)

Chris Reader: I would say that with all we have talked about, sometimes you can wonder if you've made some of the right decisions in your life..

Pam: Er, not really..

Chris Reader: But you have wondered what might have happened if you'd have done things differently?

Pam: Well, yes, sometimes..

Chris Reader: This leads me to believe that the word achievement means something to you, in as much as you have your own goals you want to achieve. These may not always seem much to other people, but they mean a lot to you. In fact, other people can tend to see you as erratic, but in fact you like change so you do things the way you see fit.

Pam: Yes I like to do things in my own sweet way

Chris Reader: Talking about this achievement thing, I would say that occasionally you can set your sights too high and can sometimes feel a little let down. Is that true?

Pam: Well, kinda.. (smiling)

Chris Reader: Sometimes you can tend to live in your own world a bit, and find yourself coming back to earth with a bump. But saying that, you do have the stamina to hit back when you need to and although some of your aspirations are a bit far fetched, you do have an uncanny knack for pulling some of them off. (long pause)

Pam: Yes, er..

Chris Reader: So I'm just having a guess here based on what we've talked about, I would say you went for a high card, like a nine or a ten. I think you probably thought of the ten of hearts.

Pam: Yes!

Chris Reader: Thanks you for being such a wonderful accomplice!

Even though this has been written up as an effect, our fictional mentalist Chris Reader uses most of the techniques we have already talked about. One very important thing he does is to make a big deal out of the choice process, creating the idea that the card that will come to Pam's mind is somehow linked to her personality and possibly her history. This guarantees that any cold reading line he may use could in some way be connected to the card, and therefore, Pam. So emphasis is placed on the 'method' which is the idea that the card that Pam picked is indicative of her personality.

Unlike simply giving someone a character reading for it's own sake, Chris did not really make too many future projections or give any kind of advice to Pam as this would have taken the effect too far from the main effect - the correct guessing of the card. Also an effect like this can never be as personal as simply 'telling someone about themselves'.

Had Chris done a 'card reading' and used the cards as some kind of oracle then of course he would have had much more scope to delve in Pam's character. But with just one card chosen, and with the need for the effect to come to a positive conclusion, he used cold reading in an appropriate manner.

If you were to use this effect, you may find yourself able to stretch the reading much further than Chris Reader. It really depends on what you're comfortable with, and how responsive your spectator is.

In this example, Chris apparently deduces the card that Pam thought of by initially reading her looks and mannerisms, and then by using the conversation itself to come to a conclusion of what Pam is like, enabling him to guess the card she chose correctly. He could have also asked Pam a series of yes/no questions and watched her reaction, or had her pick more cards out and use those as part of a greater psychological profile. He could have asked what her favourite food was and based a reading around that should he have chosen to.

It doesn't matter where you say you are getting your information from as long as it is believable and you are comfortable with it.

SECTION THREE

Other Characters, Other Lines

Beyond Stock Lines

A Final Word

Other Characters, Other Lines

One of the main purposes of this book is to get you thinking about stock lines in a new way so that you can come up with your own variations and ideas on how to memorize and elaborate on them.

The ideas behind The James Bond Cold Reading can of course be transferred quite simply to other characters. If could be that you are not as familiar with James Bond as you are with, say, Batman. It is a fairly simple exercise to take the twelve lines of the Classic Reading and create your own script lines and plot to revolve around a different character.

As long as you can come up with script lines that remind you of each original Classic Reading line, and then string these ideas together to form a plot, you can create your own. The advantage of creating your own is that they are personal to you, and therefore you will have a much easier time remembering them.

(For this reason, there is a set of flash cards that come with the James Bond references removed but the classic reading lines intact, so you can write in your own characters and scripts to learn the twelve Classic Reading lines.)

There are of course many more stock lines and truisms scattered across the cold reading literature than just the twelve Classic Reading lines. Should you wish to learn a further set of stock lines separate from the Classic Reading, it may in fact help to learn these new lines based upon a different character. You could have several characters, each with their associated stock lines, and switch between them for different people.

How about Spiderman, Forest Gump or Bill Murray in Groundhog Day? Any character you feel you know well from a movie will do. If you pick your favourite characters from your favourite movies you will already have a strong affinity for these people. This will enable you to create compelling visualizations for each one extremely quickly. Not only that, it's great fun!

Choose another ten stock lines, and see if you can pick a different character and create your own script! Don't be afraid to play with the order of the lines in order to get the best and most memorable plot. Making up your own flash cards, one for each line, is a good way to find the best order and to stimulate the process. Develop lines that connect the character to each stock line, find an order that seems to flow the best, and then create a script visualization to string the ideas together. You will be surprised just how many lines you can remember in a very short space of time.

Beyond Stock Lines

Once you have used these concepts for any length of time, you will come to see the value of the visualization. Not only does it help you remember a sequence of lines, but it can be inspirational in itself and can springboard you into all kinds of other ideas.

Think of another famous character from a film that you think you know well. Choose a multi-faceted three dimensional character such as Kevin Spacey's character in American Beauty or Jim Carrey's character in Eternal Sunshine Of The Spotless Mind. These are much richer more human and lifelike characters than James Bond.

We've seen how we can attach existing stock lines to a character, but in fact we can use just the idea of a character to extemporize ideas. Try saying ten things about Kevin Spacey's character in American Beauty NOW. Use your fingers to count them, try not to repeat yourself. Once you've done that, try it with the Jim Carrey character in the Eternal Sunshine Of The Spotless Mind film. If you don't know these characters, choose ones that you DO know. The more you empathize with a character the more you're going to have something to say about them.

What I'm talking about is coming up with your own truisms, on the spot, based upon a character that you can relate to. As I did with James Bond at the very start of this book, simply come up with statements that you think apply to the character you have in mind.

This will certainly get your brain in gear. If you practice this you will be coming up with your own truisms in no time, and with more practice you will be able to create them ON THE SPOT. Using film characters can be incredibly inspirational as they tend to have development arcs through each film which take them through the gamut of human experience. So by simply putting yourself in their shoes in any part of the movie that you may remember, you can create your own truisms for humanity in general.

Remembering film scenes in themselves can give you ideas. You may remember a character in a scene having an argument with his neighbor which could give you an idea for a line. It's not just the character's personalities that can give you ideas, it's also the situations which they find themselves in. You could even turn to book characters - the old classics have countless situations, villains and heroes that could be turned to your advantage. The Bilbo Baggins Reading anyone? Or how about the Scrooge Reading?

Whenever you're bored or killing time, try thinking of a fictional character and come up with applicable truisms for them. You can end up with a whole set of your favourite characters which you like to think about for inspiration. You may have characters which are useful for different purposes.

For instance, you can even take this a step further, and before giving someone a reading simply ask yourself, who does this person remind me of? Which famous fictional character would this person be if she had stepped out of a film? This can give you all kinds of other ideas.

A Final Word

My last bit of advice is, don't just think, speak. Practice speaking out loud. Put yourself on the spot. Think of a line and start talking IMMEDIATELY, even if it is to a wall or your car steering wheel at first. Lock yourself away, pace around the room and fire off ideas, lines and 'made up stuff' at imaginary people in imaginary circumstances. But SPEAK.

I would hate to think this was just another book about cold reading and stock lines that people read and then didn't put into practice. Without manifesting these ideas as words which come from your own mouth, you will never get started. Sometimes you will trip over your words and find it hard to work out where you're going with it all but START NOW AND IT WILL GET EASIER.

Giving readings is ten percent method and ninety percent practice. I would prefer it if you only read three pages of this book and actually started trying the ideas out, rather than reading the whole book ten times before opening your mouth.

Giving readings is about talking. Read less, talk more. Get on with it!

Julian Moore
London 2007

Download / Flashcards

You can download the flashcards that accompany this text when you register this book at:

http://thecoldreadingcompany.co.uk/coldreading/jbflash

BY THE SAME AUTHOR

CAN **YOU** REALLY LEARN TO 'READ PALMS' IN **LESS THAN A WEEK?**

~Speed Learning
PALMISTRY
PALM READINGS IN YOUR OWN WORDS

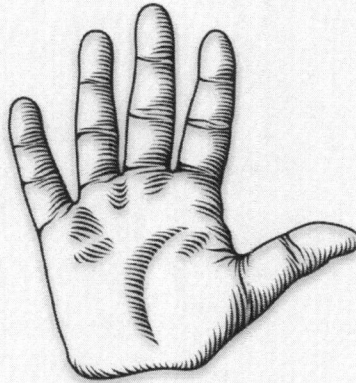

A PRACTICAL, SPEEDY PRIMER
ON THE ART OF PALMISTRY

"SPEED LEARNING PALMISTRY IS IN MY OPINION ONE OF THE BEST
MOST PRACTICAL GUIDES FOR LEARNING THIS ANCIENT DIVINATION
TECHNIQUE THAT'S EVER HIT THE MARKET"
~ CRAIG BROWNING

JULIAN MOORE

INCLUDES DOWNLOADABLE AUDIOBOOK and FLASH CARDS

BY THE SAME AUTHOR

BY THE SAME AUTHOR

Printed in Great Britain
by Amazon.co.uk, Ltd.,
Marston Gate.